This book belongs to:

Copyright © 2025 Carolyn Furlow and Amelia Furlow.

All rights reserved. No part of this book may be reproduced, stored, or transmitted by any means whether auditory, graphic, mechanical, or electronic—without written permission of both publisher and author, except in the case of brief excerpts used in critical articles and reviews. Unauthorized reproduction of any part of this work is illegal and is punishable by law.

Published by Diverse Dimensions, LLC
Illustration by FolksnFables (Team: Neethi Joseph, Jumana V.P., Indu Shaji)

979-8-9929244-0-4 (Hardback)
979-8-9929244-1-1 (Paperback)
979-8-9929244-2-8 (Ebook)

Dedication

We want to dedicate this book to all the beautiful children who realize that our relationships with animals are part of our humanity. We would also like to dedicate this book to our newest addition to our family, little Miss Avianna, who is a true bundle of joy.

"I am so excited to meet up and play with my friends at the sandbox today," Chuck said.

CRUNCH! CRUNCH! CRUNCH!

"Hey, where did all of my cookies go?"
Chuck wanted to know.

"Oh no! You ate all my cookies." Chuck cried out.

"Where did you come from?" Chuck asked. "You are so cute and fluffy." He knelt to pet the puppy.

"Do you want to come with me to the sandbox and meet my friends?" asked Chuck.

"WOOF! WOOF! WOOF!" the puppy barked as he shook his head and wagged his tail.

The puppy flew past Chuck and landed in the sandbox. He plopped and flopped headfirst into the sandbox.

SWOOSH! Sand splattered everywhere. The sand even got in Wiz's bright red hair.

Wiz yelled, "WHOAAA! What was that? My butterfly escaped!"

"OHH, NOO, my new dress got dirt all over it." Alba blurted out.

Imani screamed, "Some of my beads fell off my braids."

"Bad puppy, you got sand on everyone," Tao yelled.

The puppy walked away and hid behind a tree. Looking as sad as a puppy can be.

Everyone looked around at each other, wanting to know, "So where did the puppy go?"

"You hurt his feelings, Tao, when you called him bad," Abul said

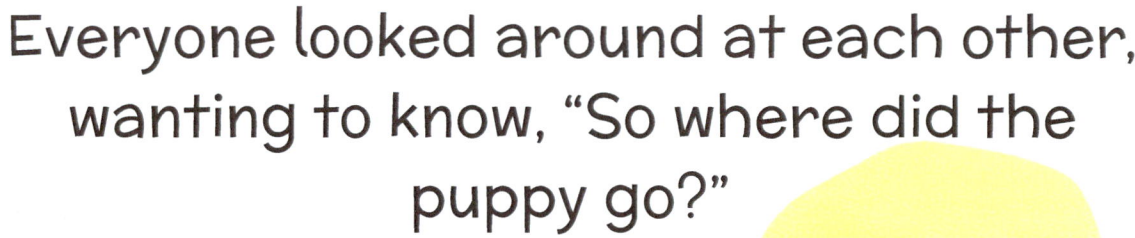

"We have to find the puppy; he is so cute," said Imani.

"He's just a little puppy; everyone makes mistakes," added Ella.

Abul said, "We all must learn to forgive each other; it is what every friendship needs."

Wiz jumped up and said, "I see him over by the trees."

"Let's go get him," said Chuck, running through the breeze.

The friends all followed Chuck for a happy run.

Just as they reached the puppy, the butterfly landed on its tongue.

The puppy stuck his tongue out and leaned towards Wiz's hand.

Wiz reached for the butterfly and put it back in his jar. "Wiz patted the dog and said, "You're a great puppy by far." "!WOOF! WOOF! WOOF!" Went the puppy.

"I'm so sorry, puppy, for what I said," Tao explained. "You are not a bad puppy; you are a good puppy."

"Aww, I love this puppy," said Imani, hugging its neck.

"I want to get a puppy, too," said Alba

Everyone agreed having a puppy would be the best thing yet.

"He can be everyone's puppy," Chuck said.

"What should we call him?" asked Wiz.

"How about Unity? Since he belongs to us all."

"Yes, Chuck, that is what he should be named."

"I am so happy to have Unity as a new friend and part of our community," Ella replied.

Everyone shouted "YAYYY and gave each other high fives."

"WOOF! WOOF! WOOF!" Unity barked.

About the author

The author, Carolyn Furlow, has a Master of Arts degree in creative writing, a Bachelor of Science in Interdisciplinary Studies, and a double minor in Psychology and African American Studies.

She is a mother and grandmother who enjoys writing and storytelling. As a teacher, Carolyn has experienced the faces of isolation of students who feel disconnected from the lessons and reading materials in their classrooms. In a spirit of love and high regard for all children, she and her daughter, Amelia Furlow, have created a series of stories that speak to all children and allow them to feel connected to the stories they read in classrooms and at home. The world is a visible melting pot of beautiful children across the globe. Our stories reflect their presence and foster acceptance and respect.

About the co-author

Amelia Furlow is currently pursuing her Master's degree in human resource management at Pepperdine University. In addition to her studies, she is a marriage and family therapy intern focusing on trauma studies, blending her passion for mental health and organizational development. With a strong commitment to personal growth and professional excellence, Amelia aims to create spaces that promote healing and understanding within individuals and organizations.

She received her Bachelor of Arts in Pan-African studies from California State University, Los Angeles. Amelia saw a need for more diverse stories in children's books. She collaborated with her mother, Carolyn Furlow, to create a series of children's books that highlight the similarities and individuality of being human. Telling stories that celebrate one's uniqueness and sameness allows children to embrace the skin they are in. Having grown up in Los Angeles, California, Texas, and Chesapeake Beach, Maryland, Amelia experienced the power of diversity at a very young age. Today, more than ever, children need to feel included. This series offers inclusiveness and brings cheer to those who read it!

www.ingramcontent.com/pod-product-compliance
Lightning Source LLC
Chambersburg PA
CBRC101014050426
42337CB00050B/67